# Cards, Cups and Crystal Ball

## A Play

### David Campton

A SAMUEL FRENCH ACTING EDITION

FOUNDED 1830

SAMUELFRENCH-LONDON.CO.UK
SAMUELFRENCH.COM

---

FOR AMATEUR PRODUCTION ENQUIRIES

UNITED KINGDOM AND WORLD
EXCLUDING NORTH AMERICA
plays@SamuelFrench-London.co.uk
020 7255 4302/01

Each title is subject to availability from Samuel French,

depending upon country of performance.

---

# CARDS, CUPS AND CRYSTAL BALL

This play was broadcast on radio in the "Afternoon Theatre" series on March 25th, 1987, with the following cast of characters:

| | |
|---|---|
| **Flora** | Rosemary Leach |
| **Dora** | Margot Boyd |
| **Nora** | Pauline Letts |
| **Lady M** | Patricia Gallimore |
| **Jessie** | Heather Barrett |

Produced by **Peter Windows**

# CHARACTERS

**Flora**
**Dora**
**Nora**
**Jessie**
**Lady M**

The action takes place in a first floor drawing room

The year is either in the last decade of the nineteenth or the first decade of the twentieth century

Scene 1  A dull morning in autumn

Scene 2  A bright afternoon in winter

Scene 3  Early evening in spring

# CARDS, CUPS AND CRYSTAL BALL

*The first floor sitting room of a Regency-style house. A dull morning in autumn*

*There is evidence of genteel poverty trying to keep up appearances— good materials worn threadbare. To the right of the room is a (possibly bow) window with a small table in front of it. There are three chairs around the table. The door is in the right of the rear wall. (Alternatively this could be an arch, with the door just out of sight round the corner.) The fireplace is in the left wall, and upstage of it there is an alcove with a screen in front of it. At an angle to the fireplace is a sofa*

*The three sisters, Flora, Dora and Nora, are sitting on the sofa. As with the room, their dresses demonstrate the art of making a little go a long way—with perhaps a suggestion that the limit has almost been reached. Flora is holding a recently-delivered letter*

*As their maid, Jessie, leaves the room, the door closes with a bang*

**Flora** Must Jessie bang the door so?

**Dora** She always does.

**Flora** We must speak to her about it.

**Nora** We do.

**Flora** Jessie has never developed into what one might call a reliable servant.

**Nora** She has become impossible since she had to wait for her wages. Beds have never been lumpier.

**Dora** Nor the porridge.

**Flora** We'd pay her tomorrow if we could.

**Nora** If only we could! ... Why don't you open the letter she brought? It may be from a client.

**Flora** It's addressed to Dora.

**Dora** You read it.

**Nora** But if it's a client ...

**Dora** There are clients and clients, Nora, dear.

*Flora opens the letter*

   (*Nervously*) Is it—?
**Flora** (*gloomily*) It is.
**Dora** Is she—?
**Flora** She is.
**Dora** Does she—?
**Flora** She does.
**Nora** We never actually promise to refund the fee if not satisfied.
**Dora** I blame the tea. How can anybody be expected to read tea-leaves with the rubbish we drink now?
**Flora** Dora, dear, you never could read tea-leaves.
**Dora** Flora, dear, that is an aspersion on my professional competence.
**Flora** You don't have any professional competence, dear. You can't read the tea-leaves any more than Nora can read a crystal ball . . .
**Nora** Really!
**Flora** . . . or I can read the cards.
**Nora** Mother could.
**Dora** Grandmother could.
**Nora** Even Aunt Esmeralda could.
**Flora** The gift appears to have passed us by. As clairvoyants we are frauds.
**Nora** Our customers are never led to expect infallibility.
**Flora** There may not be any more customers. This person is threatening to expose us. Don't fret over not being able to read the tea cups, Dora. Soon we shan't be able to afford the tea. Any more than Jessie's wages.

*The door is banged open. Jessie enters, continuing the grumble she has been having to herself while heaving the coal scuttle upstairs*

**Jessie** Upstairs and downstairs all day. How can a body be expected to run up and down stairs with a coal scuttle on little but porridge? I'd leave here . . . (*She dumps the scuttle on the hearth*)
**Dora** Would you really?
**Jessie** Only that would give certain persons an excuse for not paying certain wages. And I can tell those persons I am not

leaving here without those wages, even if I have to work here 'til doomsday.

*The distant door bell rings*

**Flora** The fire can wait a little longer, Jessie.
**Jessie** There's no more than a struggling spark left.
**Dora** The weather is quite mild.
**Nora** If we feel the cold in October, what shall we feel when winter comes?
**Jessie** With a fire in this state, madam, you'll be feeling nothing. You'll be frozen, madams all. Stiff.

*The distant door bell rings again*

**Flora** Didn't I hear the door bell?
**Dora** I believe I did.
**Nora** A client!

*The distant door bell rings again*

**Flora** Jessie—the door.
**Dora** Quickly.
**Nora** At once.
**Jessie** (*rising ponderously and lumbering to the door*) At once, madams. Upstairs and downstairs. And when I'm downstairs, no doubt you'll be wanting me to show them up . . .
**Flora** And don't slam . . .

*Jessie exits, slamming the door*

. . . the door.
**Dora** Again.
**Nora** And she left the coal scuttle.
**Flora** Again. (*She picks up the scuttle*) It *is* rather heavy. We must put it out of sight. If a client sees coal on the hearth, she may wonder why it is not in the grate.
**Nora** I suppose it *is* a client?
**Flora** Who else could it be? . . . Put this scuttle somewhere, Dora.
**Dora** (*gasping as she takes the scuttle*) It might be a friend.
**Flora** How many friends have we made in the last year? (*Pause*) Not under the table, dear.
**Dora** Then who can be coming up those stairs?
**Nora** Don't look at me. I'm not clairvoyant.

**Flora** If only you were. If only any of us were. . . . Put it behind the screen, Dora, dear.

**Dora** But if we should require our apparatus—your cards, Nora's crystal, my tea cups—the client may see. What then?

**Flora** Make believe it is a cauldron. But, Dora, dear . . . Please do not suggest your tea cups. Not today.

**Dora** But . . .

**Flora** (*moving the screen slightly aside*) Give that scandal time to settle. Perhaps the cards this time.

**Nora** Shall I fetch my rabbit's foot?

**Flora** This is no time for superstition, Nora, dear. And do put that scuttle down, Dora.

*Dora puts down the scuttle with a sigh of relief and a thump. Flora replaces the screen*

*The door is flung open as Jessie stamps into the room*

**Jessie** For you, madam.

**Flora** For me?

**Dora** Or me?

**Nora** Or me?

**Jessie** She didn't say, madam.

*Lady M enters imperiously*

**Lady M** Which of you is Miss Weerd?

**Flora** Miss Flora Weerd.

**Dora** Miss Dora Weerd.

**Nora** Miss Nora Weerd.

**Lady M** The Weerd sisters indeed!

**Flora** Whom have we the honour of addressing?

**Lady M** Why then, you had better refer to me as Lady M.

**Flora** That will be all, Jessie.

**Jessie** Huh!

*Jessie exits*

**Flora** And Jessie, don't . . .

*Too late. The door is slammed*

How may we be of service to—er—your ladyship?

**Lady M** I understand you give—consultations.

**Flora** Well ...

**Dora** We ...

**Nora** Give?

**Lady M** True or false?

**Dora** For a small fee ...

**Nora** Non-returnable.

**Flora** We have on occasion, as it were, attempted to "look into the seeds of time".

**Dora** On the understanding that too much is not expected.

**Lady M** Understood. If I waste my money, that is my business. But I'd rather you did not waste my time. You can begin now.

**Flora** If your ladyship wishes ...

**Lady M** I should not be here if I did not. How is it done?

**Flora** Cards.

**Dora** Tea cups.

**Nora** Or crystal ball.

**Lady M** Crystal balls cry out "hocus" and this hour of the morning is hardly the time for tea.

**Flora** Cards, then?

**Lady M** What else?

**Dora** Do you wish us to remain, Flora, dear?

**Nora** The other rooms being unheated.

**Lady M** Whatever the cards reveal, I prefer to learn alone. No doubt you'll tattle among yourselves. But ladies ...

**Nora** My lady?

**Lady M** To anyone else Lady M was never here.

**Dora** No, my lady.

**Nora** Never, my lady.

**Lady M** (*dismissively*) That is all.

**Dora** As your ladyship pleases.

**Nora** At once, my lady.

*Dora and Nora scurry to the door, giggling nervously and squeeze out side by side, shutting the door behind them*

**Lady M** My coachman has orders to be back at your door in ten minutes. You will be finished by then.

**Flora** Your ladyship will realize that haste is not conducive to a receptive atmosphere. (*She pulls the screen aside to reveal professional paraphernalia on shelves behind*)

**Lady M** Receptive fiddle! Is that a scuttle I see before me?

**Flora** A coal scuttle.

**Lady M** Is coal now used in making predictions?

**Flora** Very rarely. (*She hastily replaces the screen*) Will your ladyship be seated at the table?

**Lady M** As you wish. (*She sits with her back to the window*) You sit facing the light, Miss Weerd. After all, you are the performer. I am mere audience.

**Flora** Will you—shuffle the cards?

*Lady M shuffles the cards*

If I may make so bold ... I am surprised a person of your ladyship's standing should have heard of our humble establishment.

**Lady M** Very little in this part of the country escapes me. You sisters have a growing reputation.

**Flora** Your ladyship flatters us.

**Lady M** I did not say for what.

**Flora** Will your ladyship cut the cards?

**Lady M** People talk.

**Flora** They do indeed. .... Again, please.

**Lady M** I prefer to be sure of what I am talking about.

**Flora** And again.

**Lady M** Facts first; opinions later. Even in a case such as this.

*Flora begins to lay out cards on the table*

Flip-flap. Have you begun? Flip-flop. Is the oracle about to give forth? Any handsome strangers or hurried journeys?

**Flora** In good time, my lady.

**Lady M** Well—what *do* you see?

**Flora** Well—your ladyship is married.

**Lady M** Did you divine that from the cards or from my wedding ring? I am not here to be told what I know already.

**Flora** Your ladyship's carriage is emblazoned with a coat of arms. I see a bend sinister and an emblem of the chase. An old device, newly painted.

**Lady M** You might have observed as much from this window. What else do you see?

**Flora** I read that—that your ladyship—is not your ladyship: yet.

**Lady M** You mean I am not I?

**Flora** Though your ladyship is no more than a heartbeat away from the title. Or rather, two heartbeats.

**Lady M** (*half angrily, half involved*) What gossip have you been listening to? What do you know about me?

**Flora** Not knowing who your ladyship may be, how can I answer?

**Lady M** How can these pieces of pasteboard tell you that?

**Flora** They never did before. I mean—at least—not so clearly.

**Lady M** (*slightly recovered*) Continue.

**Flora** Common sense insists that, on certain subjects, a discreet reticence is advisable. Only—I—couldn't hold back. The remark came out willy-nilly. And—there's more. Pressing to be told.

**Lady M** Then tell.

**Flora** I see a father and a brother.

**Lady M** Mine?

**Flora** By marriage. The father holds the title.

**Lady M** And the brother?

**Flora** Is next in line. An earl may disinherit, but the title must always pass to the older surviving son. This particular title is about to pass. His lordship has only the feeblest grasp on life.

**Lady M** And this brother by marriage?

**Flora** Is nearer the grave than he suspects.

**Lady M** And where in the world may that grave be? Africa, America or Australia? After a lifetime of vagabonding, where is he about to come to rest?

**Flora** Where else, but in the family vault?

**Lady M** Here?

**Flora** As near here as makes no difference. He is near now.

**Lady M** The prodigal returned? I won't believe it.

**Flora** As your ladyship pleases. But a meeting is on the cards.

**Lady M** Meeting? With whom?

**Flora** With you.

**Lady M** Me?

**Flora** And him. Come back.

**Lady M** Who else do you see?

**Flora** Just you and him. Alone.

**Lady M** (*rising furiously*) Enough!

*Lady M sweeps the cards from the table and storms up and down the room. Flora picks up cards from the floor and reads them while kneeling, as though following a continuous story*

**Flora** The cards! ... Oh, my. ... Oh, my!

**Lady M** After years of presuming to be dead. Rumours constantly reaching us. How dare he rise up alive from under some foreign field!

**Flora** I see ... Oh, my! I see!

**Lady M** What do I care? What else matters? What more do you see?

**Flora** A confrontation. A confession.

**Lady M** A warning?

**Flora** Avoid old timbers and running water.

**Lady M** Cannot those cards be more specific as to time and space?

**Flora** Some details are best not revealed too soon.

**Lady M** Some details are best not revealed at all. (*With another swift change of attitude*) These deliberations are confidential, h'm? ... We had not settled on a fee. Will a guinea suffice? (*She drops a coin on to the table*) The reports of your abilities were less than flattering. I shall correct them in future. (*She glances through the window*) Don't rise from your knees to summon the servant. The stairs are dim-lit, but I can twist myself down them unaided. Understand I rely on your discretion, Miss Weerd.

**Flora** (*sitting on the floor and staring into space*) I saw.

**Lady M** Miss Weerd?

**Flora** (*with a combination of satisfaction and bewilderment*) I saw!

**Lady M** Surely the object of the experiment. I would not wish to disturb your meditation, Miss Weerd. Good day to you.

*Lady M exits*

**Flora** I saw. I saw. As plainly as print in a book. I saw.

*Dora and Nora hurry in*

**Dora** We saw her go down the stairs. Was she impressed?

**Nora** (*shivering*) I'm frozen—marooned in that dining room with no fire at all.

**Dora** Flora, dear, what are you doing down there?

**Flora** (*still not wholly aware of her surroundings*) Picking up the cards.

**Nora** How do they come to be on the floor?

**Flora** An ace of spades was only ever an ace of spades. Today it is death's visiting card. I felt a chill up my arm as I turned it.

**Dora** Have you caught a cold?

**Flora** Dora, dear—I have The Sight. It hasn't passed us by. Like Mother and Aunt Esmeralda, I have it. The how and where and why of what was revealed are still uncertain; but I am sure about the money I saw—and of the . . .

**Dora** Flora, dear,—what money?

**Nora** Do you mean this guinea?

**Dora** A guinea! Flora, you didn't say that she thought you worth a guinea.

**Flora** We only deal in danger signs—like "No Road", "Proceed At Your Own Risk" . . .

**Dora** Now we can afford some decent tea.

**Nora** We can afford to make up the fire. Where's that scuttle?

**Dora** We'll have a fire in every room.

**Nora** It's only *one* guinea, dear.

**Dora** Did anyone pay a guinea before? There'll be others. Now we have a patron in the aristocracy. What do you say, Flora, dear?

**Nora** Flora . . . ?

**Flora** There needn't actually be a murder . . .

*The Lights fade to a Black-out*

CURTAIN


SCENE 2


*A bright afternoon in winter*

*Flora stands by the table over which cards are strewn*

*The door is banged open and Jessie comes in with a tray of tea things, which she takes to the table*


**Flora** Tea, Jessie?

**Jessie** The other two madams have just come in. They'll be up directly. Stairs are no problem when a person has the use of a person's limbs.

**Flora** Still limping?

**Jessie** (*pulling up her skirt to reveal a heavily bandaged leg*)
Wouldn't anybody be limping with a leg like this?

**Flora** I'll move the cards. (*She sweeps them together*)

**Jessie** If certain persons can tell what is going to happen, why did
they not tell me I was going to fall down the front steps? If only
I'd known what I was going to do, I'd never have done it. (*She
sets out the tea things*)

**Flora** If a thing is on the cards, Jessie . . .

**Jessie** At least I'd not have left the soap where I might tread on it.

*Dora comes in, followed by Nora*

**Dora** One does not need second sight to foretell that was bound to
happen sooner or later.

**Nora** It will happen again if Jessie continues to leave objects on
the stairs.

**Dora** I almost fell over a bucket on the way up.

**Jessie** I only left it there 'til I was on my way down again, madam.

**Nora** It was there when we went out.

**Jessie** Then madam should have been expecting it.

**Flora** Did you have a pleasant walk, my dears?

**Dora** The sun was still shining, but not enough to melt the ice.

**Nora** I'm out of patience with pleasant walks. Every time a client
rings the doorbell, it's either the spare room or the Square for
us.

**Flora** A slight exaggeration, Nora, dear. And we are very grateful
for our increasing clientele.

**Dora** It is so gratifying to have tea hot and waiting. Shall I pour?

*The distant door bell rings*

**Nora** Oh, no! Not the bell.

**Dora** Not again.

**Nora** Not now.

**Flora** Nothing more has been arranged for this afternoon.

*The distant door bell rings again*

**Flora** Answer the door, Jessie, and inform whoever may be calling
that there are no consultations without prior appointments.

**Jessie** My, my. Madam is feeling her importance these days.

*Jessie goes out, banging the door*

**Dora** She doesn't bang the door *quite* so loudly now.

**Nora** I hope she takes that bucket downstairs before ...

*There is the muffled clatter of a falling bucket*

**Dora** Well, one or the other of them seems to be down.

**Nora** Jessie's manners may be uncouth; but she says what others are thinking. She's not the only one to notice madam enjoying her own importance.

**Flora** Nora, how can you utter such an untruth!

**Nora** I'm not blaming anyone, Flora, dear. You can't help feeling above us.

**Flora** But I'm not feeling above you.

**Dora** Please don't let the tea grow cold while you argue.

**Nora** Quite right, my dear. As nothing can be done to change the situation, the least said, the better.

**Flora** You have either said too little or too much. You are implying that I have changed.

**Nora** You *have* changed, dear. You are not like us any longer.

**Flora** How?

**Nora** You have something that we do not.

**Flora** Think yourself lucky I *do* have it. Remember our situation a few months ago. At least I am now able to provide for us all.

**Dora** Do we have muffins today?

**Flora** And scones. Have you forgotten when we couldn't afford even a second cup of tea? Dora, dear, do you envy me the gift?

**Dora** I'm not sure.

**Flora** Not sure, with rich Dundee on the table?

**Dora** When none of us had the gift, we were all alike.

**Flora** Exactly. All starving.

**Nora** We merely feel it unfair that one of us should have the power and not the others.

**Flora** I'm sorry, I'm sure. I'd be perfectly happy to resign in favour of you or Dora if that could be arranged.

**Dora** Once we took turns to give readings. Now we consider ourselves lucky when we are allowed to remain on the premises.

**Nora** It's cards, cards, cards all the way.

**Dora** Tea leaves are never given a chance.

**Nora** Nor the crystal.

**Flora** What do you want from me?

**Dora** When did I last read a tea cup?

**Flora** I don't know. But I can recall what happened when you did.

**Dora** Am I never to handle a tea cup again?

**Flora** We are all waiting for our tea cups now. You are about to fill them.

**Dora** Flora, dear—do let me try a reading again.

**Flora** But we are doing so well now, dear. We have a reputation. Imagine the damage one disgruntled customer could do to it.

**Nora** No one can be right every time.

**Flora** I can—on a good day. When I see nothing, I say so and arrange another appointment.

**Nora** I suggest the next appointment goes to Dora.

**Dora** Do you, Nora?

**Flora** You don't realize what you are asking.

**Nora** I do. I am asking that we behave like sisters again instead of the Fairy Queen and her attendants.

**Flora** But I never wished . . .

**Dora** We know you didn't, Flora, dear. You were our sister and . . .

**Flora** I am still your sister. . . . Fairy Queen? Oh, dear. . . . Oh, very well, Dora. For better or worse, you shall take the next caller. I promise.

**Dora** The next?

**Flora** The very next.

*The door is flung open*

**Dora** Oh, Jessie . . .

*But it is not Jessie. It is Lady M. Jessie peers round her in the doorway*

**Jessie** She wouldn't listen to a word from me, madam.

**Lady M** Your servant appears to have misheard her instructions.

**Jessie** Me? Misheard?

**Flora** Of course, Jessie. Did we not make it clear that to certain ladies we are always at home?

**Jessie** I never heard anybody say that, madam.

**Flora** (*crossing to the door*) Thank you, Jessie.

**Jessie** When did madam say that?

**Flora** That will be all.

**Jessie** When it's one order one minute and another order the next, how is a body to ...
**Flora** All, Jessie. All.

*Jessie's complaining is finally muffled by Flora, gently but firmly closing the door on her*

**Dora** An unlooked-for honour, my lady.
**Nora** An unexpected pleasure, my lady.
**Lady M** Am I truly unexpected?
**Flora** Truly, your ladyship.
**Dora** Will your ladyship take tea?
**Lady M** Milk. No sugar. I must congratulate you, Miss Weerd.
**Flora** Congratulate—me?
**Lady M** On the accuracy of your prediction. Lord M is about to make his maiden speech in the Upper House.
**Flora** How gratifying for your ladyship.
**Lady M** Not unalloyed, I fear. The old Earl's death was hardly unexpected; but it was hastened by the news of his son and heir.
**Nora** Bad news, my lady?
**Lady M** A dark night, an unsafe bridge, and a stream in spate. So near to his ancestral home too. The body was discovered by poachers. Under the circumstances they were not prosecuted over the salmon. But were you unaware of that?
**Nora** Salmon poaching lies outside our experience, my lady. (*She hands tea to Lady M*)
**Lady M** I wonder, though, that with your remarkable perception, you were not tempted to turn the page, as it were—to peek to the next chapter.
**Flora** I am not sure that would be possible without the sitter's co-operation.
**Lady M** How reassuring. (*She sips tea*) Hm. From the quality of your tea, I take it your affairs have prospered, too.
**Dora** Thank you, my lady.
**Lady M** Why thank me?
**Nora** For the recommendation.
**Lady M** Your successes act as their own advertisement.
**Flora** We try not to boast.
**Lady M** It so happens that I am troubled by a lingering doubt.
**Flora** About us, my lady?
**Lady M** Last time you said "Confrontation" and "Confession."

**Flora** If your ladyship recollects . . .

**Lady M** Every word. Poor Edward—I refer to my late brother-in-law—was cut off with no time for either. I have been left wondering. What message could have been so urgent that he braved the fatal storm to deliver it? What tidings were washed away in the torrent? . . . Well?

**Flora** I am sorry, my lady. We have no way of telling.

**Nora** We are not mediums.

**Dora** We are not in touch with your dear departed.

**Lady M** Nor am I interested in my dear departed. My concern is with the living. My cup, Miss Weerd. (*She hands it to Dora*)

**Dora** A re-fill, my lady?

**Lady M** Read it.

**Dora** Read?

**Lady M** Tea leaves are your special study, are they not?

**Flora** My sister considers herself an expert in that field. We were discussing the very subject when your ladyship was announced. Were we not, Dora?

**Dora** I wouldn't presume . . .

**Flora** No presumption, dear. Your talents are unique. Display them for her ladyship.

**Nora** Are we to withdraw again?

**Lady M** There's little advantage in that today. We all know what we know. Soon I hope to know a little more.

**Dora** My sister was so successful with the cards last time . . .

**Lady M** My cup is here. You are here. And I am here. Waiting.

**Dora** I should warn your ladyship.

**Lady M** I know that formula. You are not responsible for my future. But I need to know. What next?

**Dora** I can but do my best, my lady.

**Lady M** Best do that, Miss Weerd. What now?

**Dora** I swirl the little remaining tea in the cup, place the saucer over the cup, reverse them, replace the saucer on the table and there . . .

*Having done all that, Dora looks into the cup. She sighs*

**Lady M** Yes?

**Dora** Ah, yes, indeed.

**Lady M** What do those tea leaves tell? Does anyone living know the message my brother-in-law brought?

**Dora** Yes.

**Lady M** (*taken aback*) They do? Then who?

**Dora** His wife?

**Lady M** His—?

**Dora** His marriage was the news he failed to deliver.

**Flora** (*now regretting her little triumph*) Are you sure, Dora? A misreading at this point could have incalculable consequences.

**Lady M** Shush.

**Flora** Should I take over?

**Lady M** Enough! These interruptions are most unprofessional. Where did poor Edward acquire this wife? Is she African, Australian or an Eskimo?

**Dora** Fair haired, blue eyed and Cockney. She appears to have been a chambermaid.

**Lady M** You must be mistaken.

**Dora** She is here quite plainly—making a bed. And then, it would seem, lying on it.

**Lady M** Not even that scapegrace would smirch the family honour by . . .

**Flora** (*diplomatically*) Consider, Dora, dear. This is merely your interpretation.

**Dora** But I can see.

**Nora** You, too?

**Lady M** Where is this supposed spouse to be found?

**Dora** That I can't say, my lady.

**Lady M** Exert yourself.

**Dora** She appears to be constantly on the move. I believe in this direction. In search of her husband.

**Lady M** Were they legally married?

**Dora** It says here they were.

**Lady M** Patterns of leaves—nothing more. Do they include a reproduction of the marriage certificate?

**Dora** No need, my lady. The church is plainly here.

**Lady M** Married! Any offspring?

**Dora** Any—?

**Lady M** Did the fool beget a legitimate heir?

**Dora** He—he died childless, my lady. (*She sees something that frightens her*) Ah!

**Lady M** (*satisfied*) Ah! And . . . ?

*Dora drops the cup*

**Nora** Butterfingers, Dora.

**Flora** What a pity when you were doing so well.

**Lady M** The cup isn't broken.

**Dora** The spell is. I—can read—no more.

**Lady M** Convenient. A wife, you say. Well, that's no obstacle. She
has no claim on us—merely the widow of an elder son. The title
passed *after* poor Edward drowned. We can afford to be
generous—to a point. A son would have changed the situation.
But you are sure there is no son?

**Dora** Quite sure, my lady.

**Lady M** H'm. Yours is a very adaptable gift. It comes and goes.

**Dora** It arrived just in time this afternoon, my lady.

**Lady M** For you—or for me?

**Dora** For both of us, my lady.

**Nora** Will your ladyship take more tea? There is another cup. I
can ring for hot water, or even for a fresh pot.

**Lady M** Don't. I've done if you have. Ah. Your fee. (*She tosses
coins on to the table*) I trust you were giving me the truth.

**Dora** When the sight comes, one cannot lie.

**Lady M** Most necessary. Good afternoon.

*Nora hurries to the door to open it for Lady M*

**Dora** Good afternoon.

**Flora** Your ladyship.

**Nora** I'll hold the door open. That will shed light on the stairs.

**Lady M** You need not bother. Darkness has its advantages. I can
negotiate your dreadful stairs.

*Lady M goes out*

(*Off*) I remember their twists and turns.

**Nora** That's the worst bend, my lady. (*She closes the door and
returns to the table*) Three guineas. Three!

*She realizes that Flora and Dora are looking at each other, rigid and
unsmiling*

**Nora** Why, Flora, Dora. What's amiss?

**Flora** Dora, dear—just what were you up to?

**Dora** The sight is less of a blessing than I dreamed. I feel—most peculiar. But you are aware of that, too.

**Flora** I was aware of that, but ... What did you hold back?

**Dora** Hold back?

**Nora** You wouldn't, would you? That would amount to a breach of trust. Like taking money under false pretences.

**Dora** You've done as much in your time, dear.

**Nora** I may have embroidered when I wasn't certain ...

**Dora** Most of the time.

**Nora** But I never withheld information.

**Dora** You never had the chance.

**Nora** Don't rub that in.

**Flora** Did you, Dora? Withhold?

**Dora** No more than you, Flora, dear. When you foresaw the murder.

**Nora** Murder?

**Dora** There was no accident at the bridge, and Flora knows it.

**Flora** I advised her to avoid the bridge.

**Dora** You should have advised *him*.

**Flora** He wasn't here. If she'd heeded my warning, she'd be sleeping easier now. Without blood on her hands.

**Nora** Blood?

**Flora** A manner of speaking. No blood was actually spilled—only a lot of water. She pushed him in. Swift and simple. With no evidence or witnesses.

**Dora** Only we two.

**Flora** Our testimony would never count in a court of law. Nor would I ever wish to be one who crossed her. The title was to blame, of course. More than the money. Your ladyship! Within her grasp at last. Then he returned and would have snatched it away.

**Dora** So you must realize why I could not tell all. If she could do that to a grown man, what might she not do to a child?

**Nora** Child?

**Flora** What child?

**Nora** A lie! You know we never lie. Especially to clients.

**Dora** I did not lie.

**Nora** You insisted there was no child.

**Dora** It hasn't been born yet.

**Nora** Prevarication.

**Flora**  It will be born, though.
**Dora**  Soon.
**Flora**  And if it should be a boy . . .
**Dora**  He'll be the legitimate heir of the elder brother.
**Flora**  Then the title will pass to him.
**Dora**  Unless That One finds out.
**Flora**  Oh, my.
**Nora**  Oh, my.
**Dora**  Oh, all our mys. I do wish I'd never looked into that beastly tea cup. I wish I hadn't been able to read the signs.
**Flora**  Me, too, my dear.
**Nora**  Next you'll be telling me I'm the lucky one.
**Dora**  You are. You are.
**Nora**  You're just saying that to make me feel better about being passed over.
**Dora**  This feels like watching children at play on the railway lines.
**Flora**  With an express train due at any moment. You said the girl was making her way in this direction.
**Dora**  She knows nothing about her husband, poor thing. She is hoping to find him. If Lady M finds her first, and in that condition . . . Who needs tea leaves to foretell another "accident"?
**Flora**  We should warn her.
**Dora**  How can we do that? We can't even guess where she might be.
**Nora**  You are the ones with the powers.
**Flora**  No need to sound so resentful, Nora, dear.
**Nora**  The tea's still here.
**Dora**  No, thank you. It's stewed and cold.
**Nora**  The cards, too. Read them. (*She picks up the pack from the table and hands it to Flora*)
**Flora**  How can I read cards for a client who isn't here?
**Nora**  Read them for yourself. You are the one who wants to find the girl.
**Flora**  Me?
**Nora**  Who else?
**Flora**  Can I do that?
**Nora**  I can't do it for you. Shuffle.

*Doubtfully, Flora shuffles the cards*

*The Lights fade to a Black-out*

CURTAIN

SCENE 3

*Early evening in late spring*

*Flora and Dora are at the window. Nora is on the sofa*

*Jessie brings in a lighted lamp, which she puts on the table*

**Dora** Oh. The lamp already?

**Nora** Some people may be able to see in a glass darkly, but others need light to read by.

**Dora** I meant, is it that time?

**Jessie** It's the same time as it was at six o'clock yesterday, madam.

**Nora** You can make up the fire, too, Jessie.

**Jessie** It's only half an hour since I made it up last, madam. It's still half up the chimney.

**Flora** The room has to look specially cheerful this evening, Jessie.

**Jessie** Well, it's the madams' own money the madams are burning.

*Jessie bangs her way from the room. A few seconds later there is a muffled crash*

**Dora** What do you suppose that may have been?

**Flora** Not the coal scuttle anyway. The scuttle makes quite a different clatter on the stairs.

**Dora** And she wouldn't have complained about fetching coal if it had been up here already.

**Flora** The atmosphere must be just right. We have to break the news so very gently. Are the smelling salts handy?

**Nora** I took care of that. The only thing you'd trust me to do. Do come away from that window. The girl won't be here any quicker for all your gazing.

**Flora** It is not every day we inform a young mother that her son is a lord.

**Dora** Will she be walking here, do you think, or will she have a conveyance?

**Nora** Do you mean there's something you two don't know?

**Dora** (*sitting next to Nora on the sofa*) Please try not to feel so cut off, Nora, dear. After all, two sisters with the gift are more than we had any right to hope for.

**Nora** One sister less than I hoped for.

**Flora** Here's a carriage. I do believe it is stopping. Isn't this exciting?

**Nora** Huh!

**Dora** Don't look so glum, Nora. Even you must feel excited—face to face with the girl after all this time. Can you see her yet, Flora? What does she look like? Is the baby with her?

**Flora** But it isn't ... Oh, Gemini! That's Lady M down there.

*Nora and Dora jump up*

**Dora** (*crossing to the window*) What can she want?

**Nora** I've a good idea—without consulting the cards or tea leaves. She wants to know how much we know.

**Dora** We mustn't tell her.

**Nora** And if she demands a reading?

**Flora** We can't refuse.

*The distant door bell rings*

**Dora** She's at the door.

**Nora** Say we're not at home. That's one lie everybody is expected to tell.

**Dora** Suppose she wants ...

**Flora** As she will.

**Dora** Can you—? Can I—? Can we—?

**Flora** If she insists on a consultation, Nora must fetch out her crystal ball.

**Nora** Nora hasn't looked into her crystal for so long, I believe she's forgotten how.

**Flora** This is no time for uppity airs, dear. You can make up any tarrididdle you like without affecting any code of honour.

**Nora** Can I indeed!

**Dora** You've always done so before.

**Nora** Such flattery!

**Flora** Please, dears. Please!

*Jessie ushers in Lady M*

**Jessie** The lady, madam, that you're always at home to. I hadn't forgotten, you see. And I haven't forgotten the fire, either.

*Jessie goes out again, banging the door*

**Lady M** So. We four meet again.
**Flora** We are a little late for tea, my lady.
**Dora** Are we a little too early for a glass of cordial?
**Lady M** Miss Dora Weerd . . .
**Dora** Oh.
**Lady M** I have a grave, but I hope unfounded, suspicion.
**Dora** H'm?
**Lady M** That at our last seance information was withheld.
**Dora** I told your ladyship the truth. Nothing but the truth.
**Lady M** But was it the *whole* truth?
**Dora** Anything I may have neglected to tell your ladyship, I assumed your ladyship knew already.
**Lady M** I knew nothing about the boy.
**Dora** The boy had not been born then.
**Lady M** Ah. So you do know about him now.
**Flora** Your ladyship also?
**Lady M** I employ eyes and ears besides yours. The girl was reported as unsuspecting her late husband's station in life. Hopefully she remains in that blissful state.
**Flora** Does your ladyship know where the girl may be now?
**Lady M** Don't you?
**Flora** At this precise moment I can truthfully say no.
**Lady M** Ignorance is a great leveller.
**Dora** Indeed.
**Lady M** She is near—searching for the man we buried last winter. But exactly where?
**Flora** If only we knew.
**Lady M** That is what we shall investigate now. You sisters and myself together. Search, and maybe we shall find.
**Flora** Nora . . .
**Nora** The crystal, my lady?
**Lady M** Why not?
**Nora** At once.

*Nora draws aside the screen and takes her crystal to the table while Lady M is still talking*

**Lady M** And this time I insist on uncensored revelations. No holding back because I might already know, or ought not to know, or might not even want to know. I'll be the judge of what is relevant, Miss Weerd. I'll sift the seed from the chaff. You merely report—everything.

**Nora** (*sitting*) As well as I may, my lady. Will your ladyship be seated?

**Lady M** Were you expecting me?

**Nora** (*breathing on, then polishing her crystal*) This has not been used for some time.

**Lady M** If not me, who *are* you expecting?

**Nora** If your ladyship will concentrate her mind . . .

**Lady M** (*sitting*) Her ladyship's mind is already concentrated wonderfully.

*Nora breathes in deeply several times, exhaling with a low, slow, "Ah"*

Is that wheezing strictly necessary?

**Flora** For Nora, yes, my lady.

**Dora** With the crystal, a gentle trance is of great assistance.

**Nora** Ah!

**Lady M** Was that another sigh, or has the quarry been sighted?

**Dora** The response is seldom as prompt as this, my lady.

**Flora** Though I believe my sister realizes how urgently your ladyship needs to be on your way.

**Nora** (*as if picking up her cue*) Ah. Ah.

**Lady M** That sounded like a view halloo.

**Nora** (*overacting rather heavily*) Ah, yes. Yes. Yes, yes, yes.

**Lady M** Don't keep the message to yourself, woman.

**Nora** (*portentiously*) Blossom hangs heavy on the cherry and children play at the river's brink.

**Lady M** What has that to do with me?

**Nora** Darkness falls on castle walls.

**Lady M** Gibberish!

**Flora** She'll have news of the girl. *Soon.*

**Nora** (*her tone changing*) The—girl . . .

**Lady M** Yes. What of the girl?

**Nora** I see—a—young woman. Corn coloured hair. Cornflower blue eyes. The child's hair is like sunlight on a wheatfield.

**Lady M** Poetic babble. Where?

**Nora** (*her voice flat and toneless*) The girl trudges twilit streets, the bundle in her arm wrapped in a black fringed shawl.

**Lady M** Circumstantial evidence.

**Nora** Searching for a house. One particular number. She does not know the district. Even the town is strange to her.

**Lady M** But which town?

**Nora** Numbers are erratic as Avenue becomes Walk becomes Close becomes Square becomes Crescent.

**Dora** (*nervously*) So like this Crescent.

**Lady M** Indeed.

**Dora** Oh!

**Flora** (*shocked*) It can't be!

**Dora** (*equally shocked*) She wouldn't!

**Lady M** Why not?

**Nora** (*trancelike*) A passing lamplighter offers help. He traces these streets each evening. There is a piece of paper. The girl is reluctant to part with it. That letter is important to her. A matter of life and death, it says.

**Flora** Do you know what you are doing, dear?

**Lady M** Do *you*? Are you wilfully distracting her?

**Flora** Impossible.

**Dora** She's in a real trance. There's nothing we can do. Is there?

**Flora** Not now.

**Nora** The lamplighter points out a house. Very close.

*The door is banged open and Jessie enters with the coal scuttle*

**Jessie** Madam ...

**Lady M** (*furiously*) Not now!

**Jessie** Madam required me to make up the fire.

**Lady M** Stand still.

**Jessie** Can I put the scuttle down?

**Nora** The girl looks up. The very place—with an abandoned brush on the steps to the front door.

**Jessie** So that's where it went. ... Sorry, madam.

**Dora** It may not be here. It may not be now.

**Nora** She climbs the steps and rings the bell.

*The distant door bell rings. There is a stunned silence. Then the ring is repeated*

**Lady M** Will you not answer the door?
**Jessie** The fire . . .
**Lady M** Can wait.
**Jessie** Yes, my lady. At once, my lady.

*Jessie hurries out, taking the scuttle with her*

*Nora gives a frightened cry*

**Lady M** What? Further revelations?
**Nora** Black plumes tossing on black horses as the funeral plods towards a family vault. With armorial bearings—bend sinister and an emblem of the chase. An expensive display for so few mourners.
**Lady M** A personage of rank and title. Is this cortège past or future?
**Flora** Your ladyship knows best.
**Lady M** Who knows what?
**Flora** We all know what we know. I mean . . .
**Dora** What's done is done. I mean . . .
**Flora** Three trips to the graveyard. I mean . . .
**Dora** Two already and one to come. I mean . . .
**Flora** Father, son and . . .
**Nora** Within the week.
**Flora** What is to become of the child, my lady?
**Lady M** You may rely on me to take care of the little lordship.
**Dora** You wouldn't dare!
**Lady M** Dare? What would I not dare?
**Flora** I am sure there is nothing your ladyship would not dare.
**Lady M** Let me remind you gipsies of the law against defamation. Certain Acts of Parliament forbid witchcraft.
**Flora** But we never . . .
**Lady M** No doubt protecting an over-gullible public against fraud. You saw nothing.
**Flora** We saw nothing.
**Lady M** You suspect nothing.
**Dora** We suspect nothing.
**Lady M** You will say nothing.
**Flora** }
**Dora** } *(together)* We will say nothing.

NaN the good of your health, I prescribe an immediate change of climate. Anywhere but here.

*Jessie enters*

**Jessie** Madam, there's a person and child below.
**Flora** Show them up.
**Lady M** No need. From now on they'll be my special charge. My carriage will be waiting. You thought it a hearse, you say. I wonder why.

*Lady M's voice recedes as she sweeps from the room*

**Flora** Jessie, the lamp. Show her ladyship . . .

*A cry is mingled with a crash as Lady M takes the stairs at one step*

**Jessie** (*at the door*) Oh, madam. She's in a heap in the hall.
**Flora** The coal scuttle?
**Jessie** (*coming back into the room*) I was waiting to make up the fire.
**Dora** Go down to her. Quickly.
**Flora** We'll come, too.

*Jessie goes out*

**Nora** (*in her normal brisk voice again*) No need. A broken neck is a broken neck. I saw it about to happen.
**Dora** You didn't warn her.
**Nora** I did what I could. What more could I have done? She'd never have believed me.
**Flora** You really saw—all of it?
**Nora** I wish I hadn't. It's worse than vertigo—peering into the abyss. I feel terrible.
**Flora** Yes, dear. That's exactly the way it is. A very mixed blessing. We wanted to tell you, but you'd never have believed us.

*Jessie rushes back*

**Jessie** Oh, madam and madam and madam . . . She's . . .
**Flora** We know, Jessie.
**Jessie** The girl pale as death itself with baby crying—poor half-starved thing.

**Dora** That, Jessie, is the present Earl.

**Jessie** An Earl in the hall and her ladyship at the foot of the stairs! What is to happen next?

**Nora** (*picking up the crystal*) We could find out ...

**Dora** (*taking it from her*) The usual way.

**Flora** Exactly. We'll wait and see. (*She takes the crystal from Dora and replaces it on the table*)

CURTAIN

# FURNITURE AND PROPERTY LIST

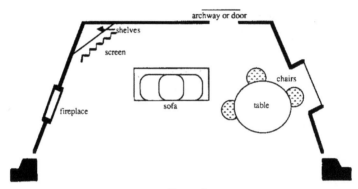

## SCENE 1

*On stage:* Small table
Three chairs
Fireplace
Screen. *Behind it:* shelves with "professional paraphernalia"
Sofa
Window curtains
Dressing at director's discretion

*Off stage:* Coal scuttle **(Jessie)**

*Personal:* **Flora:** letter
**Lady M:** bag containing money

## SCENE 2

*Strike:* Coal scuttle

*Set:* Cards on table

*Off stage:* Tray of tea things **(Jessie)**

*Personal:* **Lady M:** bag containing money

## SCENE 3

*Strike:* Tea things

*Off stage:* Lamp **(Jessie)**
Coal scuttle **(Jessie)**

# LIGHTING PLOT

One interior setting throughout

Practical fittings required: table lamp

SCENE 1

*To open:* Dull morning light. Autumn

*Cue* 1    **Flora:** "... actually be a murder."      (Page 9)
           *Black-out*

SCENE 2

*To open:* Bright afternoon light. Winter

*Cue* 2    **Flora** shuffles cards      (Page 18)
           *Fade to Black-out*

SCENE 3

*To open:* Early evening. Spring

*Cue* 3    **Jessie** brings in lamp      (Page 19)
           *Increase lighting to cover lamp*

# EFFECTS PLOT

MADE AND PRINTED IN GREAT BRITAIN BY
LATIMER TREND & COMPANY LTD PLYMOUTH
MADE IN ENGLAND